SPIRITUAL

EXERCISES

SPIRITUAL
EXERCISES

MARK
YAKICH

PENGUIN POETS

PENGUIN BOOKS
An imprint of Penguin Random House LLC
penguinrandomhouse.com

LIBRARY OF CONGRESS CATALOGING-IN-PUBLICATION DATA
Names: Yakich, Mark, author.
Title: Spiritual exercises / Mark Yakich.
Description: New York : Penguin Books, 2019. | Series: Penguin poets
Identifiers: LCCN 2019002878| ISBN 9780143133278 (paperback) | ISBN
    9780525505037 (ebook)
Subjects: | BISAC: POETRY / American / General.
Classification: LCC PS3625.A38 A6 2019 | DDC 811/.6--dc23 LC record available at
    https://lccn.loc.gov/2019002878

Printed in the United States of America
10 9 8 7 6 5 4 3 2 1

Set in Goudy Oldstyle Std
Designed by Elyse J. Strongin, Neuwirth & Associates

In Memoriam

Ann Barker

James Yakich

Marjorie Yakich

CONTENTS

I

II

III

Teach us to give and not to count the cost.

—IGNATIUS OF LOYOLA

I

After forty years I discover

I am the son of a nun
the product of
more passion
than guilt
more love
than proof
When she gave me
away she felt
everything
Now she is
working clods
light parts under bark
flowers of the
unmeasurable tree
no meter for grief
like that growing
inside
me

Sister Christopher
1937 – 1997

SON OF A NUN

There's the front door
Through which she never came, and the winter
Coat she wore while pregnant with me.
And here's the mourning I fail
To euphemize. My day-old head clipped
From a Polaroid and taped inside a locket.

I've got no pet names, birthday cards,
Or knotted strands from a blond afro
In a black hairbrush. But this
Much is true: Had we ever met,
I'd have kept even her belly button
Lint and ragged toenail clippings.

I have but her habits: hyper-tidiness,
Afternoon gin and tonics, midlife
Panic attacks. I keep meaning to frame
A photo of myself, eyes closed,
Simply to see what she might have
Looked like in the coffin.

But they say there's no need.
If I want to bring her back, I just have to
Put two fingers to my wrist
And face the heartbeats. I prefer
Hands at my throat, scratching carefully
And hard as one does a lottery card.

FORMS OF LOVE

As if each of us is the sole

Architect of our achievements.
The mind, the metaphoric

Heart, the genitalia—

All our soft animals piecing
Together can-do truths.

Praise be, then, for Mother's Milk,

Baby Daddy, and busy days
Ahead so easily forgotten.

And praise the body that goes,

That lameness shall also
End. Lovers, dice, edible

Thistle: Be unashamed.

Those selves we are
So full of are full of holes.

POST-CONFESSIONAL

You mustn't cry. You mustn't vomit.
You mustn't blame yourself for getting pregnant.
You mustn't gorge at buffets
Or swill from paper bags. You mustn't cheat.
You mustn't lie. You mustn't regret
Signing the documents
Giving your infant son away.
You mustn't not pray.
You mustn't go numb until numbness becomes
You. You mustn't get high on heroin,
Glue, gasoline, or whatever is under the sink.
You mustn't write in a diary with a flimsy lock.
You mustn't beat your breasts because the left is larger
Than the right. You mustn't drive all night to cross an imaginary border.
You mustn't sleep out in the woods in rain or snow or sun.
You mustn't go lesbian.
You mustn't become a missionary
Abroad. You mustn't throw out the rosary,
Urge the father to take you back, or pretend
For very long that nothing happened.
For over the years, you mustn't let go
Because doctors keep telling you so.
You mustn't jump. You mustn't hang.
You mustn't climb. You mustn't wonder if or when
Your son will search for you in his free time.
You mustn't orchestrate the reunion.
You mustn't hope for the day
He finds your grave
And gives God hell for the gift of sacrifice.
You mustn't trifle.
You mustn't die. You mustn't believe
There is or is not an afterlife.

AGAPE

Right before you arrived,
           she drew a bath with extra soap, wanting
      to make sure her body
               was supremely clean.
It didn't matter because in the hospital
           they made her wear two gowns.
      When she began to scream
               from the pain,
they said to focus on something else
           in the room. On the wall opposite,
      there was a small horse
               in a landscape
painting. When it was all over,
           she asked who the artist was.
      The nurses said they'd never
               noticed it before.
When she was alone, she got out
           of bed to see. It was a print titled
      And the Ass Saw the Angel Kissing.
               What do you wish
to hear, my son? She did what she could.
           But it was God who painted you
      on the world like tears down
               the face of a clown.

BABY DADDY SONG

That infant on your chest
Sleeps. No matter the noise
Machine & nest of plush toys,
He'll soon cry himself awake.

The one you kiss & caress
& sing to. The one who can't yet
Smile at his own shit. The singular
One who looks like all the rest.

That infant will grow & grow
Until you have to buy him a big-boy
Bed, pack loads of sack lunches
& keep him out of trouble.

Maybe he'll need dental braces,
A trumpet & Canadian meds.
Maybe one of his angelic fingers
Will finger a girl or a gun. This

Infant on your chest, who looks
Up to you now, his sky & favorite
Star, someday he'll discover who
You were & who you really are.

ECHO

"What's it called when somebody
Doesn't believe in God?" Daughter asked.

"Oh, that just means they forgot," Father said.
They stepped around the little pet's grave.

"I can't wait to die," she said.
"What?" he said.

"Why?" he said.
She patted the soil.

"So that I can tell John Waynes how much I like his films."
"Oh," he said.

And she pressed harder,
And later refused to wash her hands.

HE MASTERS THE CHILD PROOF LOCK AFTER A BRIEF STRUGGLE

ROSARY

FROM *THE BOOK OF HOURS*

When Son looks up at the sun,
He says he can't help thinking

That the light on his face is
Both ancient and new—

The light having taken millions
Of years to reach the sun's surface

And then only eight more minutes
To get to his eyes. "In other words,"

Father says, "there's no past
As remote as the recent past."

"No, Dad," Son says, "it's just that
When you die maybe it won't

Be any worse than my eyes
Blinded for a moment by a star."

EPISTEMOLOGY

And Daughter said, "Only girls are allowed in my room."
And Son said, "I love Momma, not Daddy."

And Momma said, "You can love Daddy, too."
And Daughter and Son said, "No!" and "No!"

What's knowledge without logical transition
Sentences? What's guilt sprung from the back

Of the hand? What love we all have for each
Others' faces and buttocks. Appreciate with

All your heart the love that runneth from
The penis, the justice that greaseth the great

Vaginal walls. Mother, you shined in the bedroom.
Father, you were always too tired to carry on

An affair. Nothing has an ideal form, and no
Child wants to get caught being too good.

LEST YOU DROVE YOURSELF FROM YOUR OWN DOOR

Worked by pushing your kids
To work harder. Got to work once
Even though the car was wrecked
Backing into one of our bikes.

Later, bankrolled one of our
Pregnancies and got arrested
Because of a windshield tinted
The color of your skin . . . O Momma,

Didn't you know that under
The wrapping papers, we'd always
Assumed there was a gift . . .
And that behind your eyelids,

We'd hoped there was a dream?
You should have told us
You were allergic to gold;
We would've forgiven you for
Not wearing a wedding ring.

BOUND

She wanted to know the difference between one man and another,
  she said to the pillow, and asked what it wanted to know.
The pillow said it wanted to know how to get rid of the bed, that it was
  tired of its company.
That's a real problem, she said. She supposed the pillow, quiet again,
  would go on lying.
But the pillow said, I can't take you for a friend because while you must
  be interested in pillowness,
which you could find nowhere better than right here in the bed,
  I'll bet you're just as interested
in sheetness, which you can find in a pure form right over there—a pure
  form of evil, if you ask me.
I know, she said, I want to be friends with you both. But the pillow
  slumped into a deep grief and said,
If you could just remove the headboard and let everything fall toward
  the wall, I might be able to escape.
Why, she said, don't I ask the bed if he wouldn't mind moving away
  from the wall enough so that you
both have more room? After all, you both enjoy my body and the
  impression I leave; surely the bed will understand sharing . . .
Not likely, said the pillow. That, she said, is ungenerous and
  unforgiving—what could you give the bed
in return for moving a little? What could I give him? the pillow said,
  and then said nothing.
Should I simply keep my eyes closed while you do whatever it is
  you're going to do? she said.
Before the pillow could answer, her lover rolled over to her side,
  his hands cupping her waist, his cock hard
and getting harder. She reached back and pulled on it, thinking it was
  some kind of sign that the bed would
never let the pillow alone. But it wasn't a sign, or it was a sign like
  everything else is a sign, in name only.

THINGS SAID TO BE INEFFABLE

A book decorates
A nightstand

And a body
Decorates a bed.

The nightstand
May be made

Of plastic, metal,
Or wood,

And is normally
The same

Height as the bed.
Even if they are

Very married,
Lovers tarry

And aver
And aver and

Tarry. Finally
One of them

Rises
To search

The dictionary
For a word

The other has
Made up.

BIBLICAL

Just shy of the surface, fish rise
And die, gleaming more
Beautifully when belly-up.

The moon kisses the sun's ass;
God sees to it. Loneliness,
My child, isn't so big after all.

Take faithful Job: In the end,
He got back a wife and children,
Just not the same wife and children

He began with. Nothing's ever
Too wrong or right. Go ahead,
Hold your breath as long as you can.

Once the fig leaf falls off,
All metaphor is disgusting.

WHY A PERFECTLY GOOD, ALMIGHTY, ALL-KNOWING GOD PERMITS EVIL

Perhaps no pleasure is greater
Than being left alone,

Which may be why whatever
It is that one wants

To call or not call God
Has little desire to be anything

Other than by itself,
A subject with no need

For the direct object
We would like to be,

A mouth without a word,
But an existence

Everywhere
By word of mouth.

CIRCLEJERK

DIVINE COMEDIES

Alone.
Alone in bed.
Alone in bed, natural causes.

Alone in a meadow, crushed by felled pine.
Alone in the woods, after running from grizzly, tripped over log, always
    at night, skull smashed on rock.
Botulism.

On the couch, suffocated with teddy bear by husband.
On the couch, smoke-drunk, throat full of puke.
On the couch, struck by meteor of sizable dimension.

On the couch, unidentified illness.
On the kitchen floor, choked on olive pit.
Choked on under-masticated slice of salami.

Choked on walnut shell.
Choked on cherry tomato, golden.
Trapped in grain silo.

Trapped in remote cave with vermin, after breaking leg.
Mown down by best friend on ski slope; moguls.
Sepsis.

In a car at the bottom of a lake.
With loved ones in a car, at the bottom of a lake, watching them go first.
After a barroom fight, boozed, cirrhotic.

Shot, randomly in the French Quarter.
Shot, by unknown assailant.
Shot, with gun purchased for the purpose of self-infliction.

Shot, easily and without thought.
Shot, left shoulder grazed, then shot again.
Overdose.

Heatstroke, hiking country roads, third day of vacation.
Strangled with silk or wool scarf, depending on the season.
Everest.

Misadventure; cell phone, cliff.
Misadventure; child, cliff.
Bird strike.

Run down by autobus, streetcar, or truck carrying fresh fish.
Complications from diabetes, appendicitis, or face transplant surgery.
Melanoma on cheeks and scalp.

Uncontrollable nosebleed.
Mudslide; humanitarian mission in Tajikistan.
Odorless gas.

Botched colonoscopy.
Drowned in storm drain after flash flood.
Asphyxiated due to buildup of deodorizing aerosol in a confined space.

Bark scorpion bite, rabid dog bite, shark bite, near infinite number of
    fire ant bites.
Cardiac arrest after severe exhaustion in hammock.
Misadventure with lawn mower and cigar.

Broadsword; schizophrenia.
Lightning strike in Central Park during oral sex with gigolo.
Anaphylaxis caused by bee sting or chickpea.

Cancer of colon, esophagus, liver, or lungs.
Cancer of tongue, pancreas, prostate, ovaries, breasts, or brain.
Rectal cancer; starvation.

Pulverization by immense object, such as construction crane ballast.
Terrorist bombing.
Drone, collateral damage.

Decapitation by helicopter propeller.
Multiple strokes.
Stabbing and blood loss caused by shank, pencil, or chopstick.

Mule.
Bear mauling while on the lam.
Cattle or bison stampede.

Avalanche.
Accidental lead poisoning.
Arsenic or cyanide.

Cannibalism; undisclosed business trip.
Rusty razor blade; lockjaw.
Baseball to the temple or chest.

Influenza, diphtheria, malaria.
Plane crash over Atlantic, Pacific, Arctic, or Indian Oceans.
Plane crash on tarmac; fire engines directed to incorrect runway.

Aneurysm.
Mercury poisoning due to taking temperature with antique thermometer.
Dysentery.

Hot-air balloon malfunction after sudden squall.
Ingested toothpick; peritonitis.
Multiple-car crash on I-55.

Huffing.
Fork, toaster: electrocution.
Tasered by law enforcement.

Hernia, complications from surgery on.
Falling coconut while retiring in Guam.
Assassination.

Extensive burns, tourist rocket launch failure.
Paper cutter.
Lethal injection.

Waterskiing disaster with boat, buoy, and small boy.
Lost at sea.
Castaway.

Lost.
Lost.
Lost.

MY FAITH

Twice upon a time,
Like a fish up a tree,
Applaudable in its failure.

PARENTING FROM CHICAGO TO ABU DHABI

By cutting each grape into eighths,
I protect small children from probable death.

Too few people are prepared
To do this. Yet one must not be afraid

To smuggle a plastic knife on board
A 787. It may be by design that I adore

The children. But I won't complain
About my life's station

Or the depth of my pocket protector
Fathoming. Because someday

These children shall perhaps
Outgrow a need for minced grapes,

And I'll be discarded as all things
Made—well or not—in China.

AUTISM

Our daughter never puts her mind on display,
Like a jewel too precious to own, or an animal
Too wild to cage. At church she's able to sit still,
But then for weeks rattles off the names of poisonous
Snakes and admonishes us that *Knowledge lies
Only outside of Creation*. She stops playing in the yard
Because the tomatoes have turned to apples,
And tells this truth to dinner guests as though
It's a family secret. At night, she sings her brother
To sleep with words like *inchoate* and *caliginous*.
And when she loves, you had better pay more
Than attention, because she does it like a curse
And will punish you simply for bearing witness.

MARRIAGE

Whereas you can never truly
Hold your own hand. Whereas

Thieves work better in pairs.
Whereas it's difficult to hold hands

And handguns at the same time.
Whereas difficult, not impossible.

A SONG MEANS LITTLE WITHOUT SEPARATION

Hardly ever
Did I blow your brothers

In my mind—all three
At once? I didn't let anybody inside me

You hadn't already abandoned.
So now I'm returning to our old kingdom,

To lay our miscarried son
On the surface of the pond

We dug for him last July.
And I will step into him like

A canoe. Don't try to stop
Me. If we float

I'll write
Again; if not, goodbye.

LOVE POEM FOR EX-WIFE

Everyone has a story
He's tired of telling.

For example,
A child dies and

It's as natural
As a flower blooming.

And a plane crash is,
As you once said,

Just a "plain crash"—
No more absurd

Than a bouquet
Of fresh-cut flowers.

But, love, never deny it—
Nature's an asshole.

When I retire
I'm going to camp out

In the backyard,
Every other night,

And dream
Of fucking you.

OBJECT LESSON

His six-year-old finally opened the bathroom door.
Dripping wet, she held out a towel. "It's beautiful, Dad.
But it doesn't work very well. It belongs in a museum."
She was right. He'd just thrown out the old towels

And bought new ones, with stunning, intricate patterns
Of loops and arabesques in bright beige and sea green.
But they were too smooth on both sides and would
Need dozens of washes before they'd feel okay.

A week later his daughter, naked, leaving a trail of water
Down the hall through the dining room and into the kitchen,
Stood before him: "Where are all the towels?"
He'd returned them to the store, but told her he'd mailed

Them off to the children's museum. "Why did you do that!"
"You said they were too pretty," he said. "I meant
They shouldn't be touched by anyone except me."
He looked into her eyes, as though they were not

Part of her face, and led her by the hand to the bedroom,
To the walk-in closet filled with his ex-wife's clothes.
"Use whatever you like but this," he said, reaching
For the nightgown. "It's silk and won't absorb a thing."

PATHSTHATCROSSFORSUCHABRIEFTIME

PATHSTHATFOREVERMAKEUSTURNANDLOOKBEHIND

YOUSEEWHATYOUWANTTOSEE

UNORIGINAL SIN

Does everybody feel like a kink
        in the evolutionary chain, or was that merely us
                post-coitus at the All Seasons Inn?

At the tail end of sex you didn't climb
        out of my body; you entered it deeper as I pulled away.
                Booty, you said, *glorifies gravity*.

When I told you I was appalled
        by your God, you asked me to strip in front of
                the Gideons, open to Romans 12:1,

Offer your bodies as a living sacrifice,
        holy and pleasing. When I told you I was afraid of
                the sunrise, you said *The sun never rises—*

only people do. That was the moment
        I loved only you. We were old,
                but we liked to watch the young

lovers from behind stained curtains
        at the outdoor café, because they left us nothing
                more than platitudes to say.

NAIVE CONVICTION

Somewhere a millionaire lover is leaving you,
Even if you're the one flying closer to

The speed of sound in the other
Direction. You might offer

To hike your *pantalones* up and down or sit hard
On his face, periodically interlarding

All the Spanish you can remember.
But he's not going to do you on his leather

Office divan. It's too expensive.
If you want unmitigated affection,

Go to the bank and stand underneath the cameras.
(Don't wear a bra.)

Or call Momma while watching soft porn on TV.
(Tears often require technology.)

Whatever you do, don't extend
Your neck like a defeated mime and don't send

In a rhyme to do a bitch's work. Anal sex
Works best if the body beats the mind to it.

LOVE POEM FOR EX-HUSBAND

It's true
That when our daughter died
I mended a hole
In my favorite dress
But then didn't wear it to sit shivah.

It's also true that for a year
I wrote and wrote and wrote
Until my teeth hurt
From sucking on pills and candies.

But now there are only
Two truths (no lie) left to me:
I enjoy riding men in a blond wig
Made out of her hair;
And I'll go to hell before
I'll give you back her dumb dog.

ANTIDEPRESSANTS

The mosquito in the room buzzes.
It is Berryman without a tranquilizer.

The poet's quarrel with himself
Turned out to be a battle with a god

Gone to seed. I, too, feel
The moron. No more sobbing

On the top stair. No more delirious
Laughter when the dive

Doesn't happen. Kingdom come
Is here for this delicate bug and I

Shall smash it in order to have
Someone else's blood on my hands.

They say that to walk
In another's shoes first requires

They are wearing shoes.
They was probably a cobbler.

Life is and is and is suddenly
No joke. The Bhagavad Gita says,

Do a thing not seeking its fruit.
Does that mean I should

Lick my fingers or simply
Wipe the blood away?

RETREAT

One mustn't imprison mystery in a phrase.
But after ten days of silence I'm pretty good
At pushing daylight around with the curtains.

And I now understand that the way to my wife's
Heart is through the clothes dryer, setting
The knob to permanent press for seventy minutes.

Songs of anguish and songs of splendor often
Sound exactly the same, and the snoring of
An ocean usually puts us to sleep. But it pains me

That I still haven't learned how to swim, carry
A tune, or grasp how I evolved into such an ass.
Maybe evolution had nothing to do with it.

FOR MY DAUGHTER

I should have taught you that it's easier
To forgive a malignant person than a malignant tumor.

I should have taught you to undo hate
By the minutes spent with relatives in peace and quiet,

By the blanks nobody knew were empty.
Sometimes the obvious stated with clarity

Has consequences. Speak when broken.
Ache when opened. The best one can

Say about the world is: *Author Unknown*.
Still, I try following the path of Sister Gertrude Morgan,

Picturing God nearby in order to keep me
Far away from you. If you ever feel

The need to talk to me again, I grant
You permission to write any sentence you want.

HALFWAY THROUGH LIFE

We went as far as the car would take us.
      We who crossed paths with the bus
and lived the whole afternoon through.

We who used to ride bikes like horses,
      high enough on the bridle
to touch the animals' ears with our own.

We who loved our parents because
      it felt like winning a contest. Then,
for a moment winning became a terrible

noise. For a moment being a parent was
      knowing that the purpose of devotion is
oblivion, and that oblivion rests on

further tests: *It's a tumor, Dad,* we said.
      With our hands around our necks,
we didn't worry about being dramatic,

because crossing the parking lot
      made as little sense as crossing
over the Lethe. Later, we should have

told him not to worry about anyone
      seeing him cry. Those Red Cross
nurses, with their morphine boats,

went on killing the same number of moths
      as they did butterflies . . .

THERE IS NO DOUBT

Mother thought grief would be romantic,
Like euthanizing a dove with one solid crack.

It was like having to clutch an unclothed
Baby who urinates from both ends.

She imagined she'd shave her head
And run off to a seasonless island

In the Pacific. She just
Drove to the coast and wept

In the car because it stalled on
The overlook and she had to call her son.

On the day of the funeral, she expected
To be full of shame for acting

Like a machine. It was like the day
Her dentist replaced a filling and failed

To notice—until she pointed it out—
That she had a meticulous bite.

She smiled for him through clenched teeth.
It was the only time she ever felt right.

PUTAGOLDCOININYOUR
HANDSANDPRETENDTO
BITEYOURNAILSNOWSW
ALLOWALLTHOSENAILS

PRAYER

MINDFULNESS

Truthfully
There is no
True thought.

No puddle
In which to drown
A toy poodle

Without picturing
Or framing
A little old lady.

In hospice care
When my mother
Could no longer

Speak for herself,
I reminded her
Grandchildren

That all was
Okay: Excessive
Flatulence is

Harmless, mostly
Involuntary,
And cliché.

PASTORAL

The distance
Between

The old
Bedridden

Couple:
Flashes of gold

Beneath the fish-
Pond ice.

ELEGY FOR THE ENGINEER

Thank you for helping design the guidance system
That took the *Apollo* to the moon.
Thank you for creating the radar-jamming equipment
Northrop put into the F-15 fighter jet.

Thank you for the Patriot missile system
And Motorola's Iridium
Satellite phone technology,
Which was well conceived but lost a lot of money.

Mostly, thank you for telling my sister and me
That we were special when we weren't.
We still think of Mom's beloved malapropisms—
That afghani, for example, under which you laid

For months, dying of a terrible treatise.
I now know I'm allowed to say anything I want.
But there's little more to say. Do you
Remember carrying us to bed each night for years?

I want to feel my sleep again like a bear
Hug, like the return of that kidnapped
Child I once pretended to be.
But there's no more bear, no sleep,

No child's play. Thank you anyway
For telling me about the voices in your head,
Which got you fired and persisted for thirty years . . .
The astral planes . . . the leprechauns . . . the elementals

Fertilizing vegetables in your garden . . .
And the most important thing you never said
But taught me about the stars—
That their observers are equally unknown.

TROUBADOUR

When I was a boy and my fist
Would land into my father's arm,

I'd cry out, and he'd say,
Didn't hurt me none.

He's been dead nine years now,
And my work is still to try

To beat myself up
And make the pain last.

TO DREAM

To take a forty-one-day walk in the desert
And a bone-cold shower
And a very good shit.

To die taking that shit
On the outskirts
Of Nogales.

To see the dead girl's ear
As an embryo inverted
And her lungs as

The gates of clouds.
To get so tired of breathing
It's breathtaking.

HUE AND CRY

What's in a life?
　　Yesterday.

What's the point of history?
　　Today.

What in the world do you want?
　　Tomorrow.

If tomorrow were already gone?
　　Wine.

What does the arc of your life resemble?
　　I've forgotten.

A rainbow?
　　No, I'd have held on to that.

A bridge?
　　No, I'd have jumped.

A willow leaf floating on the surface of a river?
　　That's it.

Which—the leaf or the river?
　　On.

On?
　　And on and of, too.

SEASONAL AFFECTIVE DISORDER

Many tragic things can happen to a squirrel.
Like Thoreau, I've detailed them all in my journal:

Coyote and golf ball attacks, sudden-onset
Lead poisoning, anaphylactic shock, et cetera.

My tally is a tiny monument without a flag.
Or so I wrote to a couple of nature mags.

Must one face a death at the psychiatrist's?
She's there to talk to and witness

One cry on standby once a week.
Twice, if one tampers with the background ink

On the script. But to hell with pills. Friends,
Send down your scat and acorns

On my head. I can take the gravity after all—
Without it, the tears might never fall.

SOLITARY

Paranoid schizophrenics suffer
From never being bored.
So, too, with kittens and snails.

Behind prison walls, the sun
Is not a star, the moon is
Never written about,
And shit just doesn't happen.

Maybe pterodactyls never flew
And Pluto shouldn't be there.
May you live one day forever
With no knowledge of it.

MEDITATION

Jai alai is a sport involving a ball
Bouncing off a walled
Space, and everything in your body
Shall end in oncology.

When it's time to leave
This world, try not to pretend
To feel things you don't feel. And then
Try harder to pretend to be real.

CONSCIOUSNESS

I command my car only in German.
I talk with my wife only in English.
I scold our children only in Mandarin.

When I hold our first grader
In my arms, as he falls asleep,
I picture him clutching the dead

Version of me I'll never see.
My daughter—she'll clutch him
Clutching me. My wife I can't

Picture. But she must be there
In the background, breathing
Hard against a tree. When I go,

I'll remember us on vacation, riding
Here in the car, everyone looking
Out the windows, talking at once—

Except me. That's when I close
My eyes, lift my hands just off
The wheel, and try to imagine

A language without the world.

DAYENU

Beach-blaséd, titanium-dioxide-larded, windswept with mollusk dust,
　　I appreciate you, St. Joseph State Park, Florida,
　　　　and dear friend Nathan who suggested you.
Goodbye for now, brown pelicans; we'll see you in New Orleans
　　when you make a pit stop. Goodbye, trails
　　　　and sand dunes that reminded us of Leelanau,
Michigan, except for the ropes we were not supposed to limbo,
　　much less traverse. Goodbye, screened-in picnic
　　　　bench where we ate Old Bay steamed shrimp
and imagined crawfish étouffée. Goodbye, certain wildernesses;
　　even unexplored, you were sweet to us. Thank you,
　　　　dolphin couple, three-deer family, and opalescent
blue crab who lost the staring contest with my son.
　　Behold mighty mosquitoes who yet carry our blood
　　　　and make me ponder a decayed John Donne.
Praise be for citronella, eucalyptus, rosemary, and above all DEET!
　　Strange praise for boners that still grace me
　　　　first thing in the morning, as though
tines of a rake I've dumbly stepped on. Thanks be to gallberry,
　　prickly pear, and all manner of endangered botanics
　　　　I am unable to name. Farewell, exit/
entrance and Miss Catherine's crisp park ranger khakis, wrinkled
　　lips, and zealous arm-waving. I didn't for a second
　　　　think of Saint Catherine or her breaking wheel
or the million-dollar homes I'd never want to own at any cost,
　　but which we soon admired driving past.
　　　　And almighty thanks that my preteen loves to read
fantasy novels in quietude on car rides home, punctuated
　　only by my dyspepsia, and that he doesn't especially
　　　　care for prolix or fatherly advice. Selah.

EASTER

Jesus and I head down
         the beach and climb over
the rocks to go fishing.
         He thinks He knows the best
spots, but more often
         than not He doesn't.
No matter. We sit there,
         toes in the water, expecting
one of our lines to sing.
         When nothing happens,
the Holy Ghost accuses us
         of "possessing an appetite
for violence that isn't
         entertainment." It's true.
I expect the lonely children
         in town to fall into abandoned
wells. But even the popular
         children say they wish other
popular children would fall
         into abandoned wells.
Jesus calls this "empathetic
         fallacy." Later at home,
where week-old wine sits
         on the kitchen table, He
makes me understand that
         silence is best broken
by a greater silence.
         I stare at the bottle
but can't pour a drop
         in the glass. "Alcohol,"

Jesus says, "is more work
          than we're able to give it."
So we take turns gazing
          out the window at the evening
sky, the treeless yard,
          and the children still
searching the grass for eggs.
          If one of them gets stung
by a bee, part of me will
          be saddened. If none do,
part of me will be
          disappointed, too.
Monday morning I wake and see
          Jesus, faintly in the distance.
He's back at the water,
          sweeping arms side to side
in grand strokes, as if painting
          waves with the heads of
His people. It appears to be all
          the rage in paradise. But I
know He'd argue otherwise.

EMPATHY

Who knows if it works out
The way most people want?

It's a bit unnerving, for instance,
To watch someone else extract

A broken wineglass from the garbage
Disposal. Yet it's oddly satisfying to

Dig out those same shards oneself.
One by one, tenderly, until a finger's

Pricked. As a method of penitence,
It rarely soothes. As a display of

Affection, it's nearly foolproof.

CHRIST OF THE OZARKS

Because often a couple of them faint from the lashings,
It requires three Jesuses to put on *The Great Passion Play*.
Didn't you know? Cedar waxwings will wait for berries

To ripen and ferment in order to get good and high.
I shall love berries and birds and lashings. I shall pick up
Cold meds and Drano at the Promised Land Drive-Thru.

I shall go to the airport in Fayetteville to watch planes
Take off again and again, to imagine the moment after
The moment God lays me down, at last, in a grass casket.

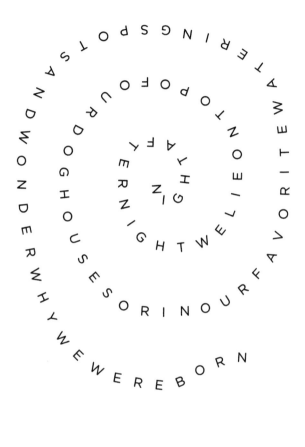

ARSPOETICA

KINDNESS

As you grow older, you think you know a little
Something about existence, like whether or not
You come from banana people. I don't believe
I come from banana people, but that doesn't mean
There wasn't a banana gatherer in the family
Generations ago. If I did come from banana people
And, say, you also came from banana people,
Would that make us treat each other better?
Would the little we know about existence
Turn out to be more or less true if our ancestors
Broke bananas together instead of bread?
I don't know. But here's a thing: Today we're
Most likely to eat one kind of banana—Cavendish—
And each comes from a clone, not a seed.

CRITICAL THINKING

When we read *A Lesson Before Dying*
We're all moved especially by the ending,
The white man asking the black man
To be his friend. One of my peers, however,
Points out how badly the female characters
Are rendered in the novel. The teacher agrees
But can't seem to find it in herself to blame
The author. There's something about literature
I'll never quite understand. Take this simile:
Hope sits on the students like sweat glistening.
It doesn't really. The AC is just out again.
And our teacher doesn't have the nerve
To tell us to wipe it off because she knows
Soon enough it'll evaporate on its own.

REFLECTION

The left eye has more floaters,
                  but it's the right eye
                      whose cornea a tennis ball
slashed forty-eight summers ago.
                  The smoke detector has blinked
                      its last blink, assuring me
that everything is conceivable.
                  The letter on the counter, for instance,
                      is stamped *Return to Sender*,
but I never mailed it. At dawn
                  I intended to walk down to the box,
                      then found myself at the end of
the jetty. As I observed my hanging
                  feet, I swear I saw an eyelash beating
                      itself between two barnacles.
An old sutra visited me:
                  Life may be a game, but if you think so,
                      you're not playing it properly.
In fact, I think I could hike
                  that mountain of waves and never return
                      if I didn't have to see it
first in my mind's eye.
                  There are only epiphanies,
                      and always have been.

ON MY OTHER MOTHER'S BIRTHDAY

Yoga master said,
Draw all your attention

To the mat.
As with all things, be present . . .

If you are cooking, cook . . .
If you are reading a book,

Read . . . And so when I visited her
Grave, I didn't bring flowers.

I got down among the fire ants
And, with car keys, cut

A pattern in the grass
So that it looked at the edges

Like frosting on a cake. I stood
In the center and pretended

To be one of fifty-nine candles.
Ants began biting my ankles,

Higher and higher they climbed,
As even breath fed the flame.

NOBLE SONG

Bells clearly rang and clouds appeared
To eat the summer grass. Tea steeped.
A window broke. The seacoast
Filled with Nova Scotia dulse.

Christmas came without presents.
Books went unread. No—to
The church. No—to the beach.
Children threw themselves on beds.

Someone rummaged the attic.
Someone preferred their ruin in the rain,
Which tasted good all the way
To the end of the pier. Everyone

Always missed the last train.
Nobody ever gathered at the piano—
Until the dying one began wailing
Not unlike a bird of prey.

REVELATIONS

When they say, Time heals all wounds,
They mean, *Worlds.*

When they say, Worlds,
They mean, *You won't even recall how much you'll forget.*

When they say, Forget,
They mean, *Someday you won't know the name of your daughter.*

When they say, Daughter,
They mean, *God.*

When they say, God,
They mean, *Eternity.*

When they say, Eternity,
They mean, *Until you are gone, too.*

When they say, Gone,
They mean, *Everyone.*

When they say, Everyone,
They mean, *We have no idea what happens after this.*

When they say, This,
They mean, *Words.*

When they say, Words,
They mean, *Meaning.*

When they say, Meaning,
They mean, *That which passes for understanding.*

When they say, Understanding,
They mean, *Peace.*

When they say, Peace,
They mean, *By which the end is justified.*

When they say, Justified,
They mean, *Amen.*

When they say, Amen,
They mean, *Say no more.*

When they say, More,
They mean, *Get on your knees again.*

When they say, Again,
They mean, *Love, Love, Love.*

NOTES

Spiritual Exercises: The title of this book is borrowed from Ignatius of Loyola, who founded the Society of Jesus (Jesuits). Ignatius was a sixteenth-century Spanish soldier turned mystic who advocated finding "God in all things" and educating the whole person in body, mind, and spirit. Originally designed for a thirty-day silent retreat, his Spiritual Exercises involve reexamining one's life through a series of prayers and contemplations.

"Forms of Love" modifies a phrase from the poet June Gehringer; thank you.

"Echo" is for Echo Matthews.

"Bound" is modeled after a poem by A. R. Ammons.

"Why a Perfectly Good, Almighty, All-Knowing God Permits Evil" borrows its opening partially from a line in a James Galvin poem.

"Divine Comedies" is inspired by Ignatius's Daily Examen, a prayer of reflection to be made at noon and at the end of the day. The idea is to become more aware of God's presence, to show gratitude, and to look forward to tomorrow. If the poem is overly prolix, one might simply recite aloud Saint Paul's dictum *I die daily* until the tongue numbs.

"My Faith" borrows two phrases from soccer color commentator Ray Hudson.

"Elegy for the Engineer" is for James Yakich.

"Dayenu" is a song of gratitude, part of Jewish Passover Seder, meaning "it would have been enough," as in "one of these gifts from God would have been enough, had there not been so many." I am indebted to Rabbi Matthew Reimer.

"Christ of the Ozarks" refers to the sixty-five-foot-tall statue of Jesus (Christ of the Ozarks) located just outside Eureka Springs, Arkansas, where *The Great Passion Play* is staged with more than 150 actors and dozens of live animals from May through October each year. The play has been performed for more than seven million viewers since beginning in 1968.

ACKNOWLEDGMENTS

Thank you to the following publications in which some of these poems previously appeared, if in different versions: *Academy of American Poets' Poem-a-Day, Adbusters, The American Journal of Poetry, The American Poetry Review, Barnstorm, Bayou Magazine, BODY, Bumf, Cellpoems, Cream City Review, Fogged Clarity, Guernica, The Offending Adam, Okey-Panky, OmniVerse, Paperbag, Ploughshares, Quick Fiction, Quiddity, Riddle Fence,* and *Saltgrass.* "For My Daughter" and "Meditation" appeared in *Liberation: New Works on Freedom from Internationally Renowned Poets* (Beacon Press, 2015), and "Troubadour" appeared in *Poem-a-Day: 365 Poems for Every Occasion* (Abrams, 2016).

Thank you to Paul Slovak, my editor at Penguin, for his continued faith in my work. Thank you to my wife, Annie, for her patience and love, especially when I least deserve it. Thank you to our children, Owen, Samara, and Jonah, without whom there would be less spirit and little exercise.

ABOUT THE AUTHOR

Mark Yakich is the Gregory F. Curtin, S.J., Distinguished Professor of English at Loyola University New Orleans.

PENGUIN POETS

PAIGE ACKERSON-KIELY
Dolefully, A Rampart Stands

JOHN ASHBERY
Selected Poems
Self-Portrait in a Convex Mirror

PAUL BEATTY
Joker, Joker, Deuce

JOSHUA BENNETT
The Sobbing School

TED BERRIGAN
The Sonnets

LAUREN BERRY
The Lifting Dress

JOE BONOMO
Installations

PHILIP BOOTH
Lifelines: Selected Poems 1950–1999
Selves

JIM CARROLL
Fear of Dreaming: The Selected Poems
Living at the Movies
Void of Course

ALISON HAWTHORNE DEMING
Genius Loci
Rope
Stairway to Heaven

CARL DENNIS
Another Reason
Callings
New and Selected Poems 1974–2004
Night School
Practical Gods
Ranking the Wishes
Unknown Friends

DIANE DI PRIMA
Loba

STUART DISCHELL
Backwards Days
Dig Safe

STEPHEN DOBYNS
Velocities: New and Selected Poems: 1966–1992

EDWARD DORN
Way More West

ROGER FANNING
The Middle Ages

ADAM FOULDS
The Broken Word

CARRIE FOUNTAIN
Burn Lake
Instant Winner

AMY GERSTLER
Crown of Weeds
Dearest Creature
Ghost Girl
Medicine
Nerve Storm
Scattered at Sea

EUGENE GLORIA
Drivers at the Short-Time Motel
Hoodlum Birds
My Favorite Warlord
Sightseer in This Killing City

DEBORA GREGER
By Herself
Desert Fathers, Uranium Daughters
God
In Darwin's Room
Men, Women, and Ghosts
Western Art

TERRANCE HAYES
American Sonnets for My Past and Future Assassin
Hip Logic
How to Be Drawn
Lighthead
Wind in a Box

NATHAN HOKS
The Narrow Circle

ROBERT HUNTER
Sentinel and Other Poems

MARY KARR
Viper Rum

WILLIAM KECKLER
Sanskrit of the Body

JACK KEROUAC
Book of Blues
Book of Haikus
Book of Sketches

JOANNA KLINK
Circadian
Excerpts from a Secret Prophecy
Raptus

JOANNE KYGER
As Ever: Selected Poems

ANN LAUTERBACH
Hum
If in Time: Selected Poems, 1975–2000
On a Stair
Or to Begin Again
Spell
Under the Sign

CORINNE LEE
Plenty
Pyx

PHILLIS LEVIN
May Day
Mercury
Mr. Memory & Other Poems

PATRICIA LOCKWOOD
Motherland Fatherland Homelandsexuals

WILLIAM LOGAN
Macbeth in Venice
Madame X
Rift of Light
Strange Flesh
The Whispering Gallery

J. MICHAEL MARTINEZ
Museum of the Americas

ADRIAN MATEJKA
The Big Smoke
Map to the Stars
Mixology

MICHAEL MCCLURE
Huge Dreams: San Francisco and Beat Poems

ROSE MCLARNEY
Its Day Being Gone

DAVID MELTZER
David's Copy: The Selected Poems of David Meltzer

ROBERT MORGAN
Dark Energy
Terroir

CAROL MUSKE-DUKES
Blue Rose
An Octave Above Thunder
Red Trousseau
Twin Cities

ALICE NOTLEY
Certain Magical Acts
Culture of One
The Descent of Alette
Disobedience
In the Pines
Mysteries of Small Houses

WILLIE PERDOMO
The Crazy Bunch
The Essential Hits of Shorty Bon Bon

LIA PURPURA
It Shouldn't Have Been Beautiful

LAWRENCE RAAB
The History of Forgetting
Visible Signs

BARBARA RAS
The Last Skin
One Hidden Stuff

MICHAEL ROBBINS
Alien vs. Predator
The Second Sex

PATTIANN ROGERS
Generations
Holy Heathen Rhapsody
Quickening Fields
Wayfare

SAM SAX
Madness

ROBYN SCHIFF
A Woman of Property

WILLIAM STOBB
Absentia
Nervous Systems

TRYFON TOLIDES
An Almost Pure Empty Walking

SARAH VAP
Viability

ANNE WALDMAN
Gossamurmur
Kill or Cure
Manatee/Humanity
Structure of the World Compared to a Bubble
Trickster Feminism

JAMES WELCH
Riding the Earthboy 40

PHILIP WHALEN
Overtime: Selected Poems

ROBERT WRIGLEY
Anatomy of Melancholy and Other Poems
Beautiful Country
Box
Earthly Meditations: New and Selected Poems
Lives of the Animals
Reign of Snakes

MARK YAKICH
The Importance of Peeling Potatoes in Ukraine
Spiritual Exercises
Unrelated Individuals Forming a Group Waiting to Cross